William HAMLET

PRINCE OF DENMARK

Text adaptation, notes and activities
by **Derek Sellen**

Editor: Rebecca Raynes
Design and art direction: Nadia Maestri
Computer graphics: Simona Corniola
Illustrations: Fabio Visintin
Picture Research: Laura Lagomarsino

© 1996 Cideb Editrice, Genoa

New Edition
© 2003   Black Cat Publishing,
               an imprint of Cideb Editrice, Genoa, Canterbury

Picture Credits
From the RSC Collection with the permission of the Governors of the Royal Shakespeare
Company: 5; Powis Castle, The Powis Collection (The National Trust) / NTPL Powis Estate
Trustees: 7; © Tate, London 2003: 74; Det Kongelige Bibliotek, Copenhagen: 92;
Bob Krist - Danish Tourist Board: 93 top; Hamlet Sommer: 93 bottom.

We would be happy to receive your comments and suggestions, and give you any other
information concerning our material. Our email and Web site addresses are:
editorial@blackcat-cideb.com
www.blackcat-cideb.com
www.cideb.it

ISBN 88-530-0012-0 Book
ISBN 88-530-0013-9 Book + CD

Printed in Italy by Litoprint, Genoa

The enhanced CD contains an audio section (the recording of the text) and a
CD-ROM section (additional fun games and activities that practise the four skills).
- To listen to the recording, insert the CD into your CD player and it will play as normal. You
  can also listen to the recording on your computer, by opening your usual CD player programme.
- If you put the CD directly into the CD-ROM drive, the software will open automatically.

SYSTEM REQUIREMENTS for CD-ROM

PC:
- Pentium™ 200Mhz processor or above
- Windows 98, ME, 2000, NT or XP
- 64 MB RAM
- SVGA monitor (800 x 600 screen resolution with thousands of colours)
- Windows compatible 24x CD-ROM drive
- Audio card with speakers or headphones

Macintosh®:
- Power PC processor or above
- Mac OS 9.0/X
- 64 MB RAM
- 800 x 600 screen resolution with thousands of colours
- CD-ROM drive 24x
- Speakers or headphones

Contents

PET Cambridge **P**reliminary **E**nglish **T**est-style exercises

T: GRADES 4/5 Trinity-style exercises (Grades 4/5)

The text is recorded in full.

The Flower Portrait of William Shakespeare by unknown artist

Shakespeare's Life

William Shakespeare was born in Stratford-upon-Avon in the English Midlands on St George's Day, April 23rd, 1564. (St George is the patron saint of England.) He was the third child of John Shakespeare, a glove-maker, [1] and Mary Arden. He went to Stratford Grammar School, where he received a good education, but he did not go to university. In 1582, he married Anne Hathaway. They had three children.

Shakespeare probably left Stratford around 1586. He joined a company of travelling actors and went to London. He became a very popular writer of plays and of poetry. Shakespeare wrote 38 plays – tragedies, comedies, histories and romances. *Hamlet*, like many of his dramas, was performed at

---

1. **glove-maker** [ˈɡlʌv meɪkə] : you wear gloves to protect/warm your hands.

the Globe Theatre in London. The Globe was very different from a modern theatre – the plays took place in the open air in daylight when the weather was good. There was no scenery [1] on the stage. [2] Boys played the female parts. Between two and three thousand people, from all classes of society, were in the audience.

When he retired from [3] writing, Shakespeare went back to Stratford and lived in a large, comfortable house called New Place. He died on his 52nd birthday in 1616 and is buried in Holy Trinity Church. After his death, some friends published his works for the first time in a book called the First Folio (1623).

If you go to Stratford, you can visit his birthplace. [4] You can also see Mary Arden's house, Anne Hathaway's cottage and, of course, the Royal Shakespeare Theatre.

Shakespeare's Times

The two centuries [5] before Shakespeare's birth were a very exciting time in history. All over Europe, new ideas were developing. People were re-discovering the culture of Ancient Greece and Rome. They explored new lands and used science to understand the world. The invention of printing (introduced into England in 1476) had resulted in more books, more studying and more knowledge. This period was called **the Renaissance**. It was the time of Leonardo da Vinci, Galileo, Erasmus and many other important people in European culture.

Hamlet is the perfect Renaissance man. He values friendship and he likes playing sport. He loves drama and playing with language and he enjoys studying and discussion. Above all, he is always thinking about life and asking

---

1. **scenery** ['si:nəri] : furniture (tables, chairs etc.) and structures to represent the time and place of the play.
2. **stage** : area in a theatre where the actors perform.
3. **retired from** : stopped (as a profession).
4. **birthplace** : the house where Shakespeare was born.
5. **centuries** ['sentʃərız] : a century is 100 years.

questions. You probably know his most famous question: 'To be, or not to be'. Shakespeare lived in the late Renaissance. England itself was changing rapidly and developing a feeling of national identity. It was a Protestant country with a powerful Queen, Elizabeth I. It was proud of its success in commerce and war. Literature, especially drama, was very important and the English language was developing all the time: 12,000 new words appeared during this time and many words were used for the first time in Shakespeare's plays.

Drama in Elizabethan England was as important as television and films today. It examined political, religious and social questions. There were many popular plays by various writers about revenge. [1] But *Hamlet* is certainly the most complex revenge tragedy of all. It is one of the plays which have made Shakespeare famous for his imagination, his use of language and his understanding of human psychology. Like Dante in Italy, Cervantes in Spain or Goethe in Germany, he is considered his country's greatest writer.

A young nobleman meditating on the meaning of life.
Edward Herbert I (1610), by Isaac Oliver

1. **revenge** : punishing someone who has maltreated you.

PET

1 Now answer the questions below.

For each question, mark the letter next to the correct answer – A, B, C or D.

1. Which of these statements about William Shakespeare is true?
   A ☐ He went to Cambridge University.
   B ☐ He married Mary Arden.
   C ☐ He left Stratford and worked in London.
   D ☐ He wrote 38 tragedies.

2. How was Shakespeare's theatre similar to a modern theatre?
   A ☐ Actors and actresses worked together.
   B ☐ There were performances every night.
   C ☐ There was a lot of scenery.
   D ☐ The actors performed on a stage.

3. What did Shakespeare do after he returned to Stratford?
   A ☐ He published his plays in the First Folio.
   B ☐ He lived in Anne Hathaway's cottage.
   C ☐ He lived in a big house.
   D ☐ He wrote many more plays.

4. When did Shakespeare live?
   A ☐ In the early Renaissance.
   B ☐ In the fifteenth century.
   C ☐ In the late Renaissance.
   D ☐ In the Middle Ages.

5. Which of the following is the best description of Shakespeare's times?
   A ☐ A period of great development in England.
   B ☐ A period when printing first came to England.
   C ☐ A period when Greece and Rome were the most powerful countries in Europe.
   D ☐ A period when Shakespeare was the only popular writer for the theatre.

Hamlet, Prince of Denmark

Hamlet is one of Shakespeare's most famous plays. It was written in 1601. *One night Prince Hamlet of Denmark meets the ghost of his dead father on the battlements* [1] *of Elsinore Castle. The Ghost tells him that he was murdered* [2] *by Hamlet's uncle Claudius. Now Claudius has married Hamlet's mother, Gertrude, and has made himself the new king. The Ghost tells Hamlet to take revenge.*

The Prince's life changes completely. He finds that the girl he loves, Ophelia, her father Polonius and even his mother the Queen all support Claudius. Everybody except his friend, Horatio, believes that Hamlet is mad. Even when he demonstrates that the Ghost's story is true, it is still difficult for Hamlet to find the opportunity to take revenge.

One disaster follows another. There is accidental murder, exile, madness and suicide. Finally, Hamlet kills Claudius. But his revenge causes many other people to die... including himself. Only Horatio survives to tell the truth [3] *to the world and to help create a new beginning for Denmark.*

Glenn Close as Queen Gertrude and Alan Bates as King Claudius in Franco Zeffirelli's film of *Hamlet*

1. **battlements** :
2. **murdered** ['mɜːdəd] : killed deliberately.
3. **truth** [truːθ] : correct information, facts.

Films of Hamlet

Many actors want to play Hamlet. Why is the role very attractive to actors? Perhaps they want to say 'To be or not to be', the most famous line from a play in the world. Perhaps they want to try to understand Hamlet's character. Perhaps they want to try to show all Hamlet's emotions – love, sadness, friendship, anger. It is a very difficult role. Perhaps they want to show that they can succeed.

There are 61 films and 21 television versions of *Hamlet*. Perhaps by the time that you read this, there will be more. Directors are always making films of *Hamlet*. I want to tell you about five films that are very famous for different reasons:

Laurence Olivier's Hamlet

Laurence Olivier was a very famous British actor. Many people still think that he was the best actor in Shakespeare plays. In 1948, he starred in a film of *Hamlet*. Olivier was also the director. It is black and white. You can see it on video or DVD. The film won two Oscars. Olivier won for 'Best Actor' and the film was also 'Best Picture'.

Grigory Kozintsev's Hamlet

This is a Russian black and white film. Shakespeare is very popular in Russia. Kozintsev made the film in 1964. A Russian actor played Hamlet. His name was Innokenti Smoktunovski. His name is difficult to remember but he was a great film actor. This is a marvellous film.

Franco Zeffirelli's Hamlet

Franco Zeffirelli is an Italian director who has made many Shakespeare films, including *Romeo and Juliet*. He used an American film star to play Hamlet – Mel Gibson. Gibson is very good. There are other famous actors in the film. Zeffirelli used Dover Castle to make the film in 1990.

Kenneth Branagh's Hamlet

Shakespeare's *Hamlet* is a very long play. The other films use only some of Shakespeare's text. But Kenneth Branagh, a famous British actor, decided to make a film of the complete *Hamlet*. It lasts four hours! Branagh is Hamlet. Many famous actors play other parts. Branagh directed the film in 1996.

Michael Almereyda's Hamlet

A Hollywood star, Ethan Hawke, plays Hamlet in this film. The director, Michael Almereyda moved the play to modern New York. The actors wear modern clothes. But the film uses the words of Shakespeare. Ethan Hawke likes Shakespeare. He also writes novels himself.

I expect that many more directors and actors will make films of *Hamlet*. Shakespeare's play is more than 400 years old but people continue to want to see it. Perhaps in 400 years from now, they will play *Hamlet* on Mars.

Top: Ethan Hawke in *Hamlet* (2000)
Bottom left: Kenneth Branagh (1996)
Bottom right: Laurence Olivier (1948)

1 Now answer these questions.

Which film of *Hamlet* do you recommend for these people? Write
Olivier/Kozintsev/Zeffirelli/Branagh/Almereyda in the box.

1. This man wants to see a modern film of *Hamlet*. He doesn't like films
   with actors in old sixteenth century clothes.

2. This girl loves old films with famous actors. She wants to see a classic
   Shakespeare film. She doesn't like American actors.

3. This boy likes Shakespeare films, but he doesn't like black and white
   films. He wants to see a film with an American star. He is interested in
   history and wants to see a film in an old castle.

4. This woman wants to know about Shakespeare. She doesn't want to see
   a film without all of Shakespeare's words in it. She likes British actors
   but she doesn't want to see a very old film.

5. This girl knows that *Hamlet* is very popular in many countries. She is
   interested in a foreign film of *Hamlet*. She prefers colour films but she
   is ready to watch black and white films.

2 Complete this table of information about the films:

Year	Director	Actor who played Hamlet	Special comments
(0) .1948..	Laurence Olivier	**(1)**	The film won **(2)** ....
(3)	**(4)**	Innokenti Smoktunovski	The film was made in **(5)** ....
1990	**(6)**	Mel Gibson	It was filmed in Dover **(7)** ....
(8)	Kenneth Branagh	Kenneth Branagh	The director used the **(9)** .... text.
2000	**(10)**	**(11)**	The film takes place in **(12)** ....

Dramatis Personae

HAMLET, *Prince of Denmark*

CLAUDIUS, *King of Denmark, Hamlet's uncle*

THE GHOST *of the dead king, Hamlet's father*

GERTRUDE, *the Queen, Hamlet's mother, now wife of Claudius*

POLONIUS, *the King's councillor*

LAERTES, *Polonius's son*

OPHELIA, *Polonius's daughter*

HORATIO, *Hamlet's friend*

ROSENCRANTZ,
GUILDENSTERN, } *courtiers and student friends of Hamlet*

Members of the King's Guard

Travelling Actors

A Sailor

A Gravedigger

Lords, Ladies and Attendants

SCENE. The Danish Royal Palace at Elsinore

Part One The Ghost

One night, at Elsinore Castle in Denmark, two guards see a ghost.

It looks like [1] King Hamlet...

But it can't be! King Hamlet is dead!

1. **looks like** :
has a similar
appearance to.

14

The next night, Horatio stays to watch with the guards. The Ghost appears again. It is wearing the same armour [1] as the old king.

1. **armour** ['ɑːmə] : metal clothes (for fighting in a war).

Prince Hamlet is very sad. His father, the King, is dead. Gertrude, his mother, has married Claudius, his father's brother. Claudius has become the new king. Hamlet does not like his uncle.

It is time to think about the future. I shall be a father to you and you will be king after me, Hamlet.

Stay here with us. Do not go back to university. We love you, Hamlet.

I shall obey you, [1] madam.

My father was a better man than Claudius. My mother was weak [2] and foolish [3] to marry my uncle.

obey [əˈbeɪ] **you** : follow your instructions.
weak : not strong.
foolish : stupid.

Horatio comes to tell Hamlet about the Ghost. Horatio has studied for many years with the Prince at university. He is Hamlet's best friend and the Prince trusts [1] him completely.

1. **trusts** : believes in. Hamlet believes Horatio is totally honest.

2. **cliff** :

Hamlet sees the ghost of his father. It signals [1] him to follow.

I am your father's spirit. If you ever loved me, revenge my murder!

Murder???

My wife, Gertrude, was unfaithful [2] to me. My brother, Claudius, murdered me. While I was sleeping in my garden, he poured [3] poison [4] in my ear.

The sun is rising. I must go. Hamlet, remember me...

1. **signals** :

2. **unfaithful** [ʌnˈfeɪθfəl] : not true in love, disloyal.

3. **poured** [pɔːd] :

4. **poison** [ˈpɔɪzən] : toxic substance.

Hamlet does not know what to do. Perhaps the Ghost is telling lies. [1]

I shall pretend to be [2] mad. Nobody will pay attention to [3] a poor crazy prince. I shall investigate my father's death.

If the Ghost's story is true, I shall kill my uncle.

1. **telling lies** [laɪz] : not giving true information.
2. **pretend to be** : give the impression of being.
3. **pay attention to** : concentrate on, think about.

1 **What happened in Part One?**

    a. Where did the guards see the Ghost?
    b. Why was Hamlet sad?
    c. Who was the new king?
    d. Why did Hamlet go to the castle walls at midnight?
    e. How did Claudius murder King Hamlet?
    f. What did Hamlet decide to do?

2 **What do you think?**

Was the Ghost telling the truth?

Was Hamlet's plan the right plan?

Comparative forms of adjectives

We use the comparative form of adjectives to compare two people, animals or things.
We form the comparative by:
- adding **-er** to one-syllable adjectives. For example: ***bigger, cleaner, darker, hotter***
- placing **more** in front of adjectives with three or more syllables.
  For example: ***more expensive***   ***more intelligent***   ***more wonderful***
- We form the comparative of adjectives with two syllables ending in **-y** like
  this: *easy* → ***easier***   *happy* → ***happier***   *lucky* → ***luckier***
- Some adjectives have an irregular comparative. For example:
  good → ***better***, *bad* → ***worse***, *far* → ***farther***, *many/much* → ***more***, *little* → ***less***
  We often make sentences with a comparative adjective + **than**.
  For example: *Hamlet's father was a **better** king **than** Claudius.*

PET **3** **Here are some sentences about *Hamlet*. For each question, complete the second
sentence so that it means the same as the first. Use no more than three words.**

    Example: Claudius is younger than Polonius.
            Polonius ..is older than................. Claudius.

    1. Claudius is a worse king than old King Hamlet.
        Old King Hamlet was .... than Claudius.
    2. Ophelia is very pretty but her servant is not so pretty.
        Ophelia .... than her servant.
    3. The weather in England is warmer than the weather in Denmark.
        The weather in Denmark .... the weather in England.
    4. Hamlet is sadder than Gertrude. Gertrude .... Hamlet.
    5. Horatio has fewer problems than Hamlet.
        Hamlet has .... Horatio.

4 Write the word from the box in the correct places on the pictures below.
(You only need ten words!)

> axe   beard   belt   boots   dagger   flag   glove   guards
> gun   helmet   knife   shield   socks   spear   sword   tie

1 `_ _ _ _ _ _`   2 `_ _ a _ _`   3 `_ _ _ r _ _`   4 g `_ _ _ _`   5 b `_ _ _`

6 a `_ _`   7 `_ _ _ t _`   8 `_ w _ _ _`   9 s `_ _ _ _ _`   10 `_ _ _ g`

Now use these letters to complete the Ghost's message:

C _ _ U _ _ U _   M _ _ _ _ _ _ _ D   M _ !

PET **5** **LISTENING**

Listen to Part One of *Hamlet* on the recording. After the bells you will hear someone talking about *Hamlet*. For each question, put a tick (✓) in the correct box.

1. Hamlet is   A ☐   happy.
                                                 B ☐   mad.
                                                 C ☐   intelligent.

2. He often   A ☐   plays games.
                                                   B ☐   acts in the theatre.
                                                 C ☐   says strange things.

3. Hamlet wants other people   A ☐   to understand him.
                                                 B ☐   to help him.
                                                 C ☐   to believe that he is mad.

4. The people want Hamlet   A ☐   to be King.
                                               B ☐   to become well.
                                               C ☐   to get married.

5. The Queen is worried because   A ☐   her son is behaving crazily.
                                                 B ☐   Hamlet is dangerous.
                                               C ☐   Hamlet saw the Ghost.

6. Who knows about the Ghost?   A ☐   The Queen.
                                               B ☐   Horatio and the guards.
                                               C ☐   Everyone, except the Queen.

6 Look at these three ghosts.

This is part of a letter you receive from an English penfriend.

> *In your last letter, you told me that you saw three ghosts. Please write and tell me more about them. When did you see them? What did they look like?*

Now you are writing a letter to this penfriend.
Write your letter in about 100 words.
Begin the letter like this.

> *Dear Beth,*
>
> *Something very strange happened to me last night.*
> *At 1 o'clock, I woke up suddenly. There was a ghost in my bedroom!*
> *It was a girl with long blonde hair. She was wearing a white dress*
> *and a yellow hat with flowers. She looked very happy and I wasn't*
> *afraid. After a few minutes I went back to sleep.*

Now continue the letter, describing the other ghosts.

Two hours later...

At five o'clock...

I know you won't believe me – but it's all true!

love from

Now *you* draw a picture of a ghost and describe it.

7 **SPEAKING**

Find a partner and talk about ghosts. For example, ask your partner:

a. Do you believe in ghosts?

b. Have you ever seen a ghost?

c. Do you like stories or films about ghosts?

d. Does your town/village have a ghost story?

e. Whose ghost would you like to meet? Shakespeare's ghost? Marilyn Monroe's ghost? Napoleon's ghost? Cleopatra's ghost?

f. What questions would you ask them?

PET 8 The people below all want to talk to a ghost. Below there are some descriptions of ghosts. Decide which ghost (A-H) would be the best one for each ghost-hunter (1-5) to talk to. For each number, write the correct letter.

1. ☐ Ben wants to talk to a ghost who can tell him about being a successful leader. He would like to meet someone who was successful during a war. He is more interested in meeting a politician from the last century than in questioning someone from earlier history.

2. ☐ Sarah is interested in powerful women. She wants to talk to the ghost of someone who was the leader of her country and succeeded in making her country better.

3. ☐ Julie is also interested in powerful women. She wants to ask someone from the past about the problems of being a leader. She wants to ask: 'Was it difficult to be a female leader? Did you fail because you were a woman?'

4. ☐ Ken believes that war is not necessary. He wants to talk to a leader who succeeded without fighting his or her enemies.

5. ☐ Sue is interested in European history. She knows that there are many famous kings and queens, emperors and generals. But she wants to question somebody from the past who succeeded in another area, for example science or art.

A CLEOPATRA'S GHOST

Cleopatra was a famous Egyptian queen. She loved Mark Antony but he died. She also loved Julius Caesar. People say that she was very beautiful, powerful and determined. However, when she lost the war, she killed herself.

B NAPOLEON'S GHOST

Napoleon was a famous general and emperor. At first, he was very successful in war and he controlled a large number of countries in Europe. However, he lost his final battle at Waterloo.

C HAMLET'S GHOST

Hamlet was a young prince in Denmark many centuries ago. His father died and his mother married his uncle. His father's ghost told Hamlet about his murder. Hamlet was in a very difficult situation.

D MARILYN MONROE'S GHOST

Marilyn Monroe was a famous film actress in the 1950s and 1960s. She was very beautiful and very successful but she was unhappy. Finally, she killed herself.

E LEONARDO DA VINCI'S GHOST

Leonardo was a famous Renaissance artist and scientist in Italy. He painted the *Mona Lisa*, a very popular painting. He also invented many things. He even had ideas for an aeroplane and a submarine.

F WINSTON CHURCHILL'S GHOST

Churchill was a British Prime Minister during the Second World War in the twentieth century. He was a very good leader. The British people loved him. He worked closely with the Americans and the Russians.

G GHANDI'S GHOST

Ghandi was a famous Indian leader. When he was alive, the British controlled India. Ghandi tried to make the British give India its independence. He believed in peace and did not agree with violence. Finally, he succeeded.

H QUEEN ELIZABETH I'S GHOST

Queen Elizabeth was the queen when Shakespeare was writing. She was a very successful queen. During the time that she was queen, England became rich and very powerful in Europe.

9 DRAMA: THE GHOST'S VISIT
Now try acting a part of the play.
Divide into groups of four students.
Give each person* one of these roles:
NARRATOR,** HAMLET, GHOST, HORATIO

- Practise speaking the lines from page 18 to page 19. Think about intonation – which are the important words in each line? Think about the emotion of each character. Hamlet is very sad. Later he is shocked. The Ghost is very serious. Horatio is calm.

- Add a few more lines at the end of the scene. What questions does Horatio ask Hamlet? For example: 'What did the Ghost tell you?' How much does Hamlet tell him?

- In each group, act the scene for your teacher and ask for advice.

- Now, each group comes to the front and acts the scene.

* Girls can take male parts if necessary. Remember that Shakespeare used male actors for female parts!
** The Narrator reads the story at the top of each page.

Part Two Hamlet and Ophelia

Ophelia lives at the castle. She has a brother, Laertes, who is studying in Paris. Ophelia is in love with Hamlet. One day, while she is sewing, [1] Hamlet comes to her room. Later she tells her father Polonius, a foolish old lord, [2] about Hamlet's visit.

1. **sewing** [ˈsəʊɪŋ] :
2. **lord** : aristocrat, nobleman.
3. **stared** [steəd] : looked for a long time.

Polonius trusts Claudius and Gertrude. He has no idea that Claudius is a murderer or that Gertrude has been unfaithful to King Hamlet.

1. **hide** [haɪd] : stay in a secret place.

Polonius gives instructions to Ophelia. He wants her to walk up and down the castle hall, reading her prayer book. [1]

1. **prayer** [preə] **book** : book of religious verses.
2. **find out** : discover.

Ophelia, you must help us find out [2] the truth about Prince Hamlet's madness.

Hamlet is thinking deeply. [1] He wants to escape from his problems by committing suicide. [2] His mind is full of questions.

To be, or not to be? That is the question. Is it better to live or die? But what happens after we die? Nobody knows.

I am stupid! I must stop thinking and *do* something. I must discover the truth.

But look, here comes Ophelia. Why is she standing there? Is it a trap?

32

1. **deeply** : seriously.
2. **committing suicide** : killing himself.

The Prince is angry with Ophelia because he realises that she is a spy for her father Polonius and King Claudius.

1. **I believed so** : I thought exactly that.
2. **nunnery** : place for nuns (unmarried women in a religious community).

The King does not believe that love is the reason for Hamlet's madness. He is very suspicious. [1]

1. **suspicious** [sə'spɪʃəs] : Claudius does not trust Hamlet.
2. **ruined** : destroyed.
3. **heavens** : divine powers.

PET **1** **What happened in Part Two?**

Look at the statements below about Part Two of *Hamlet*. Read Part Two again and decide if each statement is correct or incorrect. If it is correct, write A in the box. If it is incorrect, write B in the box.

                                                                        A   B

1. Hamlet came to Ophelia's room and told her about the ghost. ☐ ☐
2. Ophelia tells her brother about Hamlet's visit to her room. ☐ ☐
3. Polonius is a very clever old man. ☐ ☐
4. Claudius and Polonius plan to listen to Hamlet and Ophelia. ☐ ☐
5. Ophelia does not want to help them to spy on Hamlet. ☐ ☐
6. Hamlet is very happy because he has seen his father's ghost. ☐ ☐
7. Hamlet says unkind things to Ophelia. ☐ ☐
8. Claudius believes that Hamlet is mad because he loves Ophelia. ☐ ☐
9. Ophelia is unhappy because she thinks Hamlet is mad. ☐ ☐
10. Hamlet knows Claudius's secret. ☐ ☐

2 **What do you think?**

Was Ophelia right to tell her father everything?

Was Hamlet cruel to Ophelia?

3 **There are two families in *Hamlet*. Write the missing names in these family trees.**

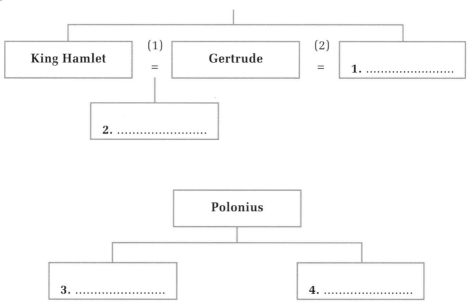

Write some sentences about the family relationships of the characters, using as many of the words in the box as you can.

Example: Polonius is Ophelia's father.

> father   mother   brother   sister   son   daughter   uncle   aunt
> niece   nephew   cousin   grandfather   granddaughter
> grandparents   step-father   husband   wife   brother-in-law
> fiancé(e)   bride   partner   girlfriend

Now write a short paragraph about the people in *your* family. If you want, you can invent the information!

Example: I have a very interesting family. My great-great-grandfather was a pirate! My aunt was a famous writer...

Present Simple and Present Continuous

We use the Present Simple to talk about things which happen *always, often, generally, usually, every week* etc.

We use the Present Continuous to talk about things which are happening *at this moment, now*.

For example: *Hamlet **lives** in the castle of Elsinore.*

*Where is Hamlet? He's **studying** in his room.*

There are some verbs which we do not use in the Continuous form. These include:

> *belong   cost   hate   have* (= possess)   *know   like*
> *love   own   understand   want*

4 **Put the verbs in brackets in the correct tense form, either Present Simple or Present Continuous.**

0. 'Where is Claudius?' 'He ..is drinking.... in the dining hall.' *(drink)*

1. Ophelia .... Hamlet. *(love)*

2. Look! Ophelia is in the hall. She .... a book. *(read)*

3. Why .... Ophelia .... ? Is she sad? *(cry)*

4. Hamlet .... Claudius. *(hate)*

5. Horatio said to Hamlet, 'Look! The Ghost ....' *(come)*

6. Gertrude is upstairs in the castle. She .... to Claudius about Hamlet. *(talk)*

7. Polonius always .... his son and daughter a lot of questions. *(ask)*

8. 'Be quiet,' said Polonius. 'The King ....' *(speak)*

9. We usually .... ghosts in the middle of the night. *(see)*

10. Look, Hamlet. Claudius and Polonius .... behind the curtain. *(hide)*

PET 5 WRITING

Polonius is a strict father. Even today, parents and children often have problems.
This is part of a letter that you receive from an English penfriend.

> My father doesn't like my boyfriend. He doesn't allow me to see him. My mother doesn't like my best friend. She doesn't let me invite her to the house. My sister is often unkind to me. Do you have problems with your family? Tell me about them in your next letter.

Now you are writing a letter to this friend.
Write your letter in about 100 words. You can invent information about your family – use your imagination!

PET 6 LISTENING

After the bells at the end of Part Two, you will hear a conversation between Hamlet and Polonius.
Look at the six sentences below. Decide if each sentence is correct or incorrect. If it is correct, put a tick (✓) in the box under A for YES. If it is not correct, put a tick (✓) in the box under B for NO.

	A YES	B NO
1. Hamlet was reading a book when he met Polonius.	☐	☐
2. Hamlet's answer to Polonius was: 'Worse, worse, worse.'	☐	☐
3. Hamlet said that the book told lies about old men.	☐	☐
4. Hamlet compared the cloud to various animals.	☐	☐
5. Polonius always agreed with Hamlet.	☐	☐
6. Hamlet said goodbye to Polonius politely.	☐	☐

INTERNET PROJECT: OPHELIA

Many artists painted pictures of Ophelia. The most famous painting is by a nineteenth century English artist, John Everett Millais (see page 74), but there are many more.

What can you find out about different artists and their paintings of Ophelia?

Use a search engine such as Google or Altavista. Enter key words.

For example: **paintings of Ophelia**. Or the **name** of an artist from the list below and **Ophelia**.

Here are six artists who painted pictures of Ophelia:

- Dante Gabriel Rossetti
- John Everett Millais
- Anna Lea Merritt
- Odile Redon
- John W. Waterhouse
- Henrietta Rae

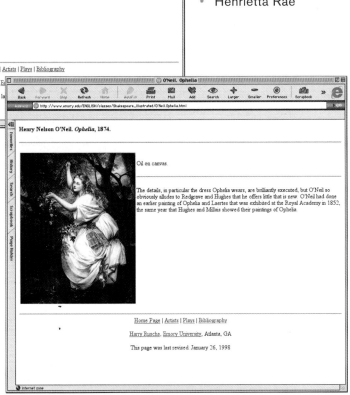

Can you find images of their paintings on the Internet?

Can you find other artists who painted Ophelia?

Print off your favourite painting and show it to other students.

Part Three The Play

Two university friends come to visit Hamlet. Their names are Rosencrantz and Guildenstern. At first Hamlet is very pleased to see them. But they ask a lot of questions and he becomes suspicious.

1. **What's the matter with you?** : What's your problem?

Some travelling actors arrive at Elsinore. Hamlet loves the theatre and he greets [1] them like old friends.

1.   **greets** : welcomes, says hello to.

We have come to perform a play for the King and Queen. .

That night, Claudius and Gertrude watch the play. There are three characters – the Player King, the Player Queen [1] and Lucianus, the Queen's lover... the murderer!

1. **the Player King ... the Player Queen** : the King and Queen *in the play.* (They obviously represent King Hamlet and Gertrude.)

All the court [1] of Denmark watch the play. Ophelia, Polonius, Horatio, Rosencrantz and Guildenstern are all there. But nobody knows the secret of King Hamlet's death... except Claudius and Hamlet. On the stage, while the Player King is sleeping, the murderer pours poison in his ear. Hamlet watches Claudius's face carefully. [2]

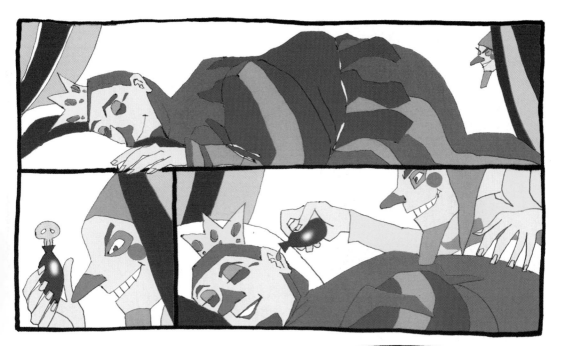

This is the Ghost's story. If Claudius is afraid, I shall know he is guilty. [3]

1. **the court** : the lords and ladies who serve the King and Queen. ('The court' is also the place where the King and Queen *live*.)
2. **carefully** ['keəfəli] : attentively.
3. **guilty** ['gɪlti] : not innocent.

After the play, Claudius feels very guilty so he goes to pray [1] in the chapel. [2] Hamlet finds him there.

1. **pray** [preɪ] : speak to God.
2. **chapel** : small church.
3. **soul** [səʊl] : spirit.

4. **heaven** : the place where God lives.
5. **hell** : the home of the Devil.
6. **repent** : be *really* sorry.

I want God to forgive me for my brother's murder. Perhaps, if I pray, he will help me.

It would be easy for me to kill him now. But if I kill him while he is praying, his soul [3] will go to heaven. [4] I want him to go to hell. [5] I shall wait for another opportunity.

I cannot repent! [6] God doesn't listen to my words!

1 **What happened in Part Three?**

  a. Why didn't Hamlet trust Rosencrantz and Guildenstern?
  b. When the actors arrived, what was Hamlet's idea?
  c. What was the story of the play?
  d. Did Hamlet watch the play carefully?
  e. Why did Claudius go to pray?
  f. Why didn't Hamlet kill Claudius?

2 **What do you think?**

Was Hamlet right *not* to kill Claudius?
What do you think will happen next?

3 **Read the definitions a-k under the picture and complete the words about the theatre.**

  a. The person who writes plays.   d r a m _ _ _ _ _
  b. The place where the actors stand.   s t _ _ _
  c. Ophelia is one of these.   c _ _ _ a c t e r s
  d. A play with an unhappy ending.   t _ _ g _ d y
  e. A play with a happy ending.   c _ m _ _ y

f. The people who watch the play.   a u _ _ O _ c e

g. The clothes for the actors.   c _ O _ _ m e s

h. You need this to go inside the auditorium. t _ _ O _ t

i. This is where you buy **h**.   b _ x   o f _ _ _ O

j. The moment when you eat an ice-cream.   i n t _ _ _ O l

k. The name of a famous Italian playwright.   O _ _ _ _ d e l l o

Now rearrange (these letters) to spell a famous name.

S h _ _ _ _ _ _ _ _

Sentences with *while*

We can join two parts of a sentence with **while**. If the actions in both parts of the sentence are long continuous actions which are happening at the same time, we use a Continuous tense. For example:

*While the actors **are performing** the play, Claudius **is thinking** about the murder.*

4 **Now look at sentences a-j. Study the example. Find pairs of sentences. Then, write 4 new sentences about the story of *Hamlet* using *while*.**

a. Hamlet and Ophelia are talking.

b. Horatio is talking about the Ghost.

c. Claudius is praying.

d. The actors are performing the play.

e. Hamlet is standing behind him.

f. The Player Queen is talking to the Player King.

g. Polonius and Claudius are listening.

h. Hamlet is watching Claudius carefully.

i. Hamlet is thinking about his father.

j. The murderer is planning to kill him.

0. While Horatio is talking about the Ghost, Hamlet is thinking about his father.

1. ....

2. ....

3. ....

4. ....

But if one part of the sentence is a short, quick action, we use a Simple verb.
For example: *While the Player King **is sleeping**, the murderer **pours** poison in his ear.*

5 Now look at sentences a-j below. Study the example. Find pairs of sentences. Then, write 4 new sentences about the story of *Hamlet* using *while*.

a. The soldiers are guarding the castle.

b. Ophelia is sitting in her room.

c. Polonius and Claudius are listening.

d. The Ghost appears.

e. The murderer is poisoning the Player King.

f. He is talking to the players.

g. Hamlet has an idea.

h. Claudius stands up.

i. Hamlet enters.

j. Hamlet is unkind to Ophelia.

0. While Polonius and Claudius are listening, Hamlet is unkind to Ophelia.

1. ....

2. ....

3. ....

4. ....

 PET 6 LISTENING

After the bells at the end of Part Three, you will hear Hamlet talking to the travelling actors. As you listen, look at the notes of one of the actors. For each question, fill in the missing information in the numbered space.

Prince Hamlet's Advice

Do not speak (1) .... or too quietly.
Do not move your (2) .... too much.
It is important to (3) ....
Remember: the (4) .... of the words is important.
Don't (5) .... to the play.
Don't change the (6) ....

7 Beth's friend Mac has just come back from a holiday in Stratford-upon-Avon. He went to see a new Shakespeare play there. Beth wants to find out about it.

romance
tragedy
comedy
history play

theatre — big/small
old/modern
a good seat

easy to understand
long
short
interesting
boring
a good ending

murder
war
love

director
actor
actress

special effects
music
dancing

Write the conversation between Beth and her friend. You can start like this:

Beth: .... (*enjoy*) the play, Mac?

Mac: Oh, yes, it was really ....

Beth: What type of play was it?

Mac: .... It was the story of ....
....
....

Beth: Did you have *a good seat* .... ?

T: GRADE 5

8 TOPIC – ENTERTAINMENT

Think of a play you've seen at the theatre, or a film that you saw at the cinema or on TV recently. Tell the class about it and why you liked/didn't like it using the following questions to help you:

a. Where and when was the story set?

b. What was the story about?

c. Who were the main actors? Were they good?

 **WRITING**

Look at this information:

Hamlet

at the Royal Shakespeare Theatre Stratford-upon-Avon
One night only: March 17th at 19.30

■

Mel Graves plays Hamlet with
Anthea Wise as Ophelia and Alan Hughes as Claudius

Special transport:
coach from Victoria Station, London:
departs 15.00 & returns to London after the performance.

Overall price:
to include transport from London,
front row seat and dinner in The Swan Restaurant: £55

This is part of a letter you receive from an English friend.

Yes, I'd like to see 'Hamlet' with you. When is it on? How much do the tickets cost? How will we get to Stratford from London? Who are the actors? Can you tell me about the play? What is the story? Write back soon, with more information. . .

Now you are writing a letter to this friend. Write your letter in about 100 words. Use these phrases to help you:

The performance starts at. . .
We've got seats in the front row.
. . . is playing the part of . . .

INTERNET PROJECT: THE GLOBE THEATRE

Many plays by Shakespeare took place at the Globe Theatre in London. The original Globe Theatre burnt down but in the late twentieth century, a group of people rebuilt it. Now, if you go to London, you can see the Globe Theatre.

What can you find out about the 'new' Globe Theatre from the Internet?

Use a search engine such as Google or Altavista and look for sites about the Globe Theatre.

Can you find the answers to these questions?

1. When did they finish rebuilding the 'new' Globe?
2. Where in London is the Globe?
3. What is the exact address of the theatre?

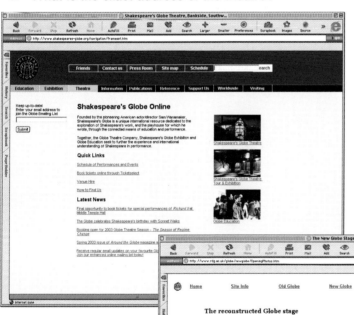

4. What is the name of the American who had the idea of rebuilding it?
5. What plays by Shakespeare are they performing this year at the Globe?
6. How much does it cost to buy a ticket to see a play?

7. Apart from plays, what can you see at the Globe?
8. Which other countries have 'Globe Centres'?
9. Which are the nearest underground stations?
10. Where can you eat and drink at the Globe?

Part Four Murder and Exile [1]

It is the middle of the night, the time for witches [2] and ghosts. Hamlet goes to see his mother in her bedroom. He does not know that someone is hiding behind the curtain [3] and listening to everything.

1. **exile** ['egzaɪl] : obligation to live in a foreign country.
2. **witches** : women who can do magic.
3. **curtain** ['kɜːtən] :

> Hamlet, why did you offend the King?

1. **Why did *you* betray** [bɪ'treɪ]...? : Why were *you* disloyal to... ?

The Queen is afraid of Hamlet and she begins to scream. [1] The spy behind the curtain shouts for help. Hamlet turns round quickly and, without thinking, kills the listener.

1. **scream** : make a loud noise. (Gertrude is very frightened.)
2. **rat** :

When Hamlet pulls back [1] the curtain, he sees Polonius... dead!

1. **pulls back** : opens.

Suddenly, the Ghost appears in the room. He has come to remind Hamlet [1] to take revenge before it is too late. Gertrude cannot see or hear him, so she thinks that Hamlet is crazy.

1. **remind** [rɪ'maɪnd] **Hamlet** : help Hamlet to remember.
2. **hurt** [hɜːt] : cause pain to.
3. **Don't waste time!** : Don't wait! Do it now!
4. **pity** ['pɪti] : feel sorry for.

The Ghost disappears.

No, I'm not mad, Mother.
Look at this portrait [1] of my father.
He was a good, brave, handsome man.
Remember him and stay away
from Claudius!

I will, sweet Hamlet.

But as soon as [2]
Claudius kisses you,
you will forget everything
and tell him my secrets.

No, I promise not
to betray you.

I am glad, [3] Mother.
Now I must take away
Polonius's body.
Goodnight.

1. **portrait** : picture (usually the head and shoulders) of a person.
2. **as soon as** : the moment when.
3. **glad** : happy.

When Claudius hears that Hamlet has killed Polonius, he decides to send the Prince away.

Hamlet is dangerous. I shall send him to England. Perhaps he will recover from his madness in a different country. Rosencrantz and Guildenstern, go with him and look after [1] him.

I shall send secret letters to the King of England. I shall tell the English to execute [2] Hamlet as soon as he arrives. When he is dead, I shall be safe.

1. **look after** : take care of.
2. **execute** : kill.

1 **What happened in Part Four?**

    a. Who and where was the spy in the Queen's bedroom?
    b. Why did Gertrude begin to scream?
    c. Why did Hamlet kill Polonius?
    d. Why did the Queen think that Hamlet was mad?
    e. What did Hamlet show to the Queen?
    f. What was Claudius's secret plan?

2 **What do you think?**

Was Hamlet right to kill Polonius?
Did the Queen know about her husband's murder?
Will Hamlet succeed in getting revenge?

3 **Look at the words in the box.**

> clever   cruel   evil   intelligent   obedient
> changeable   dependable   foolish   kind   strong
> confident   depressed   guilty   loving   unlucky
> confused   dishonest   innocent   mad

Which words would you use to describe these characters? (You can use some words for more than one person!)

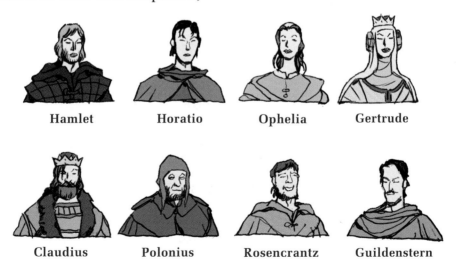

    Hamlet   Horatio   Ophelia   Gertrude

    Claudius   Polonius   Rosencrantz   Guildenstern

Can you think of any more words to describe them?

PET 4 Read Parts Three and Four again. Then answer the questions below. For each question, mark the letter next to the correct answer – A, B, C or D.

1. Why is Hamlet in a difficult situation?

   A ☐ Because his friends visit him from the university.

   B ☐ Because Ophelia is angry with him.

   C ☐ Because the Ghost lied to him.

   D ☐ Because Horatio is his only real friend.

2. Why does Hamlet put the Ghost's story on the stage?

   A ☐ Because the Players are his friends.

   B ☐ To entertain the King and Queen.

   C ☐ Because he wants to see Claudius's reaction.

   D ☐ Because the Ghost wants him to do this.

3. Why is Polonius behind the curtain in the Queen's bedroom?

   A ☐ Because he wants to spy on Hamlet.

   B ☐ Because the Queen calls for help.

   C ☐ Because he is afraid of Hamlet.

   D ☐ Because he wants to catch a rat.

4. Why does the Ghost enter the bedroom?

   A ☐ To tell Hamlet again to kill Claudius.

   B ☐ To tell Hamlet to punish the Queen.

   C ☐ To talk to the Queen.

   D ☐ To show the Queen that Hamlet is mad.

5. Which of the following is the best description of the death of Polonius?

   A ☐ A violent murder by a mad prince.

   B ☐ A good thing, because Polonius was a fool.

   C ☐ A terrible thing, because Polonius was a good man.

   D ☐ A mistake, which leads to Hamlet's journey to England.

PET **5** **LISTENING**

After the bells at the end of Part Four, you will hear a description of Hamlet's journey to England. There are seven questions in this part.
For each question, there are three pictures.
Choose the correct picture and put a tick (✓) in the box below it.

Example: Who went to England with Hamlet?

1   How did Hamlet travel to England?

2   What were Rosencrantz and Guildenstern doing?

3 What did Hamlet steal?

A ☐   B ☐   C ☐

4 What did the letter tell the person who received it to do to Hamlet?

A ☐   B ☐   C ☐

5 What did Hamlet write at the end of the new letter?

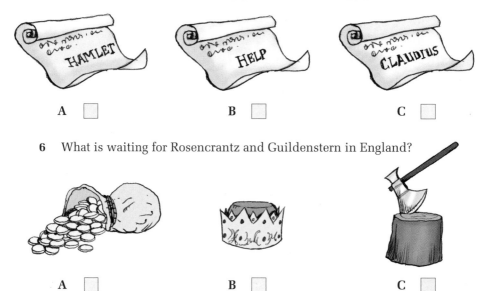

A ☐   B ☐   C ☐

6 What is waiting for Rosencrantz and Guildenstern in England?

A ☐   B ☐   C ☐

7 Hamlet wanted to go:

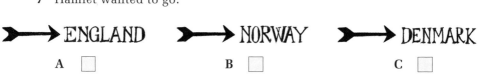

➤ ENGLAND   ➤ NORWAY   ➤ DENMARK

A ☐   B ☐   C ☐

6 MURDER AT ELSINORE!
Imagine you are a detective at Elsinore Castle.
This is what you know:

• Polonius was killed in the Queen's bedroom
• his body is missing

Who do you want to interview?

What questions do you want to ask?

Do you trust everybody? Will they tell the truth?

Write your interview with the characters.

7 A MURDER STORY
Look at these ideas for a murder story:

• Somebody killed the film star, Andrea Angel.
• Where did they find the body? In her villa? In the film studio? In the nightclub?
• Inspector Francis investigated the crime.
  What did he find? A gun? A knife? A bottle of poison?
• He interviewed some witnesses.
  Who did he interview? Her ex-husband? The film director? Another actress?
• He found some fingerprints on the gun/knife/bottle.
• He arrested somebody.
• Who murdered Andrea Angel?
  Was it her ex-husband because she left him?
  Was it the film director because she wanted to work for another director?
  Was it another actress because she was jealous of her success?

Now use some of these ideas to write a story.
Your story must begin with the sentence:

One night last month, somebody murdered Andrea Angel.

Write about 100 words.

Part Five *Suicide*

Polonius's son, Laertes, returns to Denmark from Paris. He is very angry.

Ophelia comes to see Laertes. She loved Hamlet but he killed her father. This has made her mad. She sings sad songs and gives flowers to everyone she meets.

What is the matter with my sister?

She has lost her mind, [1] poor girl.

He is dead, lady, he is dead.
He will never come again.
His beard was as white as snow.
He is gone, he is gone.
Love, remember me.

Do you see this? Oh God!

1. **lost her mind** [maɪnd] : become mad.

65

A sailor [1] brings a letter to Horatio. When he opens it, he discovers that it is from Hamlet.

> Horatio,
> I am in Denmark. Some pirates attacked our ship. While everybody was fighting, I jumped onto their ship. I paid them and they brought me home to Denmark.
> Rosencrantz and Guildenstern have continued to England. I shall tell you more about them when I see you. Meet me in the graveyard. [2]
>
> Hamlet

1. **sailor** : person who works on a ship.
2. **graveyard** ['greɪvjɑːd] : cemetery.

66

Claudius also receives a letter from Hamlet.
He has a private conversation with Laertes.

This letter is from Hamlet. He is back in Denmark.

But why didn't you put Hamlet in prison?

He is very popular with the people. It was impossible to punish him. The best thing was to send him to England.

He has killed my father and driven my sister out of her mind! [1] I would do anything to get my revenge.

I'm glad. I will kill him.

I have a better plan...

1. **driven** ['drɪvən] **my sister out of her mind!** : made my sister mad!

The Queen comes in.

I have bad news, Laertes. Ophelia is dead. She wanted to put flowers on the willow tree. [1] While she was climbing, [2] she slipped [3] and fell into the river. She floated [4] there, singing. Then she drowned. [5]

Was it suicide?

Nobody knows. Perhaps it was an accident. Oh, sweet Ophelia! I hoped she would marry Hamlet. Come, let us go and bury her. [6]

Now Hamlet has killed my father *and* my sister.

1. **willow** ['wɪləʊ] **tree** :
2. **climbing** ['klaɪmɪŋ] : moving towards the top of the tree.
3. **slipped** : lost her balance.
4. **floated** : stayed on the surface (of the water).
5. **drowned** : died underwater.
6. **bury** [beri] **her** : put her dead body in a grave.

Hamlet meets Horatio in the graveyard. They see a gravedigger. [1] He is preparing a new grave and he has uncovered some old bones. [2] Hamlet begins to talk about death.

Look at this skull, [3] Horatio. It is Yorick's. He was the court jester. [4] Alas, poor Yorick. I knew him, Horatio. When I was a child, he carried me on his back. His jokes [5] were the best. He cannot make anybody laugh now.

Perhaps this skull belonged to [6] a beautiful lady. She cannot paint her face [7] now. Perhaps this skull belonged to a lawyer. [8] He cannot show how clever [9] he is now. Perhaps this skull belonged to a court gentleman. He cannot wear elegant clothes now.

1. **gravedigger** ['greɪvdɪgə] :

2. **bones** : parts of a skeleton.

3. **skull** :

4. **court jester** [kɔːt 'dʒestə] : clown who entertained the King and Queen.

5. **jokes** [dʒəʊks] : comic stories.

6. **belonged to** : was the property of.

7. **paint her face** : put on make-up.

8. **lawyer** ['lɔɪə] : advocate, legal representative.

9. **clever** : intelligent.

1 **What happened in Part Five?**

    a. Why did Laertes want to lead a revolution?

    b. What did Ophelia do when she was mad?

    c. How did Hamlet escape from the ship to England?

    d. Why didn't Claudius put Hamlet in prison?

    e. How did Ophelia die?

    f. How many skulls did Hamlet talk about? Whose were they?

2 **What do you think?**

Was Hamlet responsible for Ophelia's death?

Did she commit suicide?

3 **Put the correct verb from the box into the sentences a-l.**
Remember to use the Past Simple.

fall	run	feel	send	fight	shake
find	sing	hide	stand	meet	think

    a. Hamlet .... against the pirates.

    b. Polonius .... behind the curtain.

    c. Hamlet .... Horatio in the graveyard.

    d. Ophelia .... into the river.

    e. Laertes and Claudius .... hands.

    f. Hamlet .... a lot about death.

    g. Claudius .... Hamlet to England.

    h. Ophelia .... sad songs.

    i. They .... her body in the river.

    j. The King .... out of the court.

    k. Hamlet .... depressed after his father's death.

    l. The guards .... on the castle walls.

4 Look at this scene with Ophelia by the river.
Choose the correct word from the box for numbers 1-12.

branch	leaves	bushes	rabbits	cloud	river
flowers	sheep	frog	swallow	grass	willow

1. s _ _ _ ◯

2. _ ◯ _ _ d

3. _ _ _ _ c ◯

4. _ ◯ a _ _ _

5. ◯ _ _ _ _ _ w

6. _ _ _ _ ◯ _ _

7. _ _ _ _ _ ◯ tree

8. _ _ _ _ _ ◯ s

9. _ _ ◯ _ _

10. b _ _ _ ◯ _

11. _ ◯ _ _ _

12. _ r ◯ _

Now use (these letters) to make a title for the picture:

S _ _ _ _   O _ _ _ _ _ _

5 What other English words about the countryside and nature do you know?
Add more words to the tables:

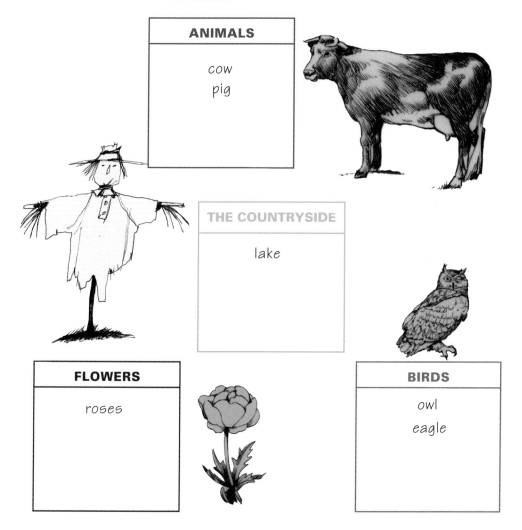

ANIMALS
cow
pig

THE COUNTRYSIDE
lake

FLOWERS
roses

BIRDS
owl
eagle

T: GRADE 4

6 TOPIC – WEEKEND ACTIVITIES
Find a picture of an activity/hobby that people usually do at the weekends
or think about an activity that you normally do at the weekend.
Tell the class about this activity using these questions to help you:

a. Where does the activity take place?

b. Do you need any special training or knowledge to do this activity?

c. What type of equipment do you need?

d. Is this activity limited to a certain age group?

7 **Here is a poem based on Shakespeare's language.
Read it carefully. (Use a dictionary to help you.)**

There is a willow by the river.
Its silver leaves shine in the glassy water.
Ophelia walked there, picking the flowers
to hang on the graceful branches of the tree.
But as she was climbing up to the sky,
a thin branch broke under her small feet
and she fell down into the weeping [1] brook. [2]
Her dress spread wide [3] and, like a mermaid, [4]
she floated on the surface, singing old melodies.
She was as happy as a creature of the water
but as her clothes grew heavy, they pulled her down
to the dark bottom of the river, to muddy [5] death.

John Everett Millais, *Ophélie* (1852)

1. **weeping** : crying.

2. **brook** [bruk] : small river.

3. **spread** [spred] **wide** :

4. **mermaid** :

5. **muddy** : mud is a mixture of earth and water.

Now listen to the Queen, after the bells at the end of Part Five. Cover the poem on page 74 and fill in the spaces.

There is a .... by the river.

Its silver leaves .... in the glassy water.

Ophelia walked there, ... the flowers

to hang on the .... branches of the tree.

But as she was .... up to the sky,

a thin branch .... under her small feet

and she fell .... into the weeping brook.

Her dress spread .... and, like a mermaid,

she floated on the ...., singing old melodies.

She was as .... as a creature of the water

but as her clothes grew ...., they pulled her down

to the dark .... of the river, to .... death.

8 Here are some opinions about the characters in *Hamlet*. In each box, write

A if you agree

D if you disagree

? if you are not sure...

1. Ophelia is a weak person. ☐

2. Ophelia loved her father more than she loved Hamlet. ☐

3. Everybody feels sorry for Ophelia. ☐

4. Laertes is a good son and brother. ☐

5. Laertes trusts Claudius too easily. ☐

6. The Queen loves Hamlet. ☐

7. Polonius was responsible for his own death. ☐

8. Hamlet was lucky to escape death in England. ☐

9. Claudius is the cleverest person in the story. ☐

10. Horatio does not help the situation. ☐

9 WRITING: LIFE STORY

In the graveyard, Hamlet picks up four skulls and imagines four people's lives. Here are some more skulls:

gangster   actor/actress   tennis champion

millionaire   doctor

Here are some questions which help us to imagine the life of the actress.

What was her name?
Where was she born? When?
When did she become an actress?
When did she make her first film?
How many films did she make?
How many Oscars did she win?
What was her most famous film?
Who did she act with?

Was she married? How many times?

Did she have children?

Where did she live?

Was she always successful in her career?

When did she die? How old was she?

 **Your English teacher has asked you to write a story.
Your story must begin with the sentence:**

This is the life story of ...., *a famous* ....

Write about 100 words.

10 DRAMA: OPHELIA'S DEATH

**Now try acting a part of the play. Divide into groups of four students. Give
each person* one of these roles:**

NARRATOR,** CLAUDIUS, LAERTES, GERTRUDE

- Practise speaking the lines from page 68 to page 69. Think about
  intonation and stress – which are the important words in each line? Think
  about pauses in the speeches. Think about the emotion of each character.
  Laertes is very angry. Claudius is very cunning (= clever). Gertrude is very
  sad.

- Add a few more lines at the end of the scene. Perhaps Gertrude says:
  'Hamlet was mad. It was an accident.' Perhaps Laertes says: 'I cannot
  forgive him.' Use your own ideas.

- In each group, act the scene for your teacher and ask for advice.

- Now, each group comes to the front and acts the scene.

---

*   Girls can take male parts if necessary or boys can play females. Remember that Shakespeare
    used male actors for female parts!

** The Narrator reads the story at the top of each page.

Part Six The Rest is Silence

While he is standing in the graveyard, Hamlet sees a procession approaching. It is Ophelia's funeral. The Queen throws flowers into the grave

and says, 'Sweets to the sweet.' Hamlet did not know that Ophelia was dead.
He is shocked. He jumps into the grave and fights with [1] Laertes.

1. **fights with** : attacks.

Laertes wants his revenge. He and Claudius decide how to kill Hamlet.

You must challenge [1] Hamlet to a fencing match. [2] He loves this sport. He will certainly agree.

Yes, and I shall put poison on the tip [3] of my sword. If I cut him, he will die.

And if this plan fails, I shall give Hamlet a poisoned drink.

1. **challenge** : invite (to fight).
2. **a fencing match** : Claudius suggests a match with swords.
3. **tip** : end.

Hamlet accepts the challenge. He does not know about the poisoned sword. To him, the fight is just [1] sport — something he enjoys!

I am sorry for your father's death, Laertes.

I accept your apology, Hamlet. Now, let's begin the fight.

Here is a drink for you, Hamlet, if you are thirsty. Good luck to you! I have bet [2] six horses that you will win.

1. **just** : only.
2. **bet** : risked. Claudius will give six horses to Laertes if he wins. Laertes will give six horses to Claudius if Hamlet wins.

Hamlet fights well and scores [1] the first points. The Queen is very happy. She picks up [2] the cup of poison. Claudius tries to stop her drinking – but it is too late!

1. **scores** : wins.
2. **picks up** : takes (in her hand).

Laertes wounds [1] Hamlet with the poisoned sword. Later, in the confusion, they exchange swords [2] and Hamlet wounds Laertes. The poison enters their blood.

1. **wounds** [wuːndz] : cuts.
2. **they exchange swords** : Hamlet takes Laertes's sword and Laertes takes Hamlet's.

Suddenly, the Queen screams in pain. Laertes falls to the ground and Hamlet begins to feel weak. The poison is working.

1. **The King is to blame** : The King is responsible.
2. **Treason!** : The lords and ladies of the court accuse Hamlet of a crime against king and country (because they don't know that Claudius killed Hamlet's father).

Hamlet is dying. Polonius, Ophelia, Laertes, Gertrude and Claudius are all dead. It is time for a new beginning in Denmark.

1. **flights of angels** : groups of flying angels.
2. **thee** : you (object).
3. **thy** : your.
4. **And ... rest** : this line comes from Shakespeare's original play. (Here, 'And' means 'I hope that ...'.)

PET 1 **Look at the statements below about Part Six. Read Part Six again to decide if each statement is correct or incorrect. If it is correct, write A in the box. If it is incorrect, write B in the box.**

A B

1. Hamlet expected to see Ophelia's funeral in the graveyard.
2. Laertes is very angry with Hamlet.
3. Laertes plans to use a poisoned sword.
4. Hamlet wants to kill Laertes, so he agrees to fights with him.
5. Claudius has a second plan to kill Hamlet.
6. The Queen drinks because her son is winning.
7. Claudius stops Gertrude from drinking.
8. Before he dies, Laertes tells Hamlet the truth.
9. Hamlet wants to be king, so he kills Claudius.
10. Everyone from two important families in Denmark is dead.

2 **What do you think?**

Were all the deaths necessary? Who was to blame?

3 **Use the verbs from the box to fill in the gaps in sentences a-k. (Make sure that you use the correct form!)**

> break   marry   bring   rise   drink   see   hear
>
> take   know   throw   leave   write

a. Gertrude .... her brother-in-law.
b. The Ghost disappeared when the sun ....
c. After Hamlet .... the Ghost, his life changed.
d. Claudius .... Rosencrantz and Guildenstern to Elsinore.
e. Laertes .... Paris as soon as he .... the news about Polonius.
f. On the ship to England, Hamlet .... the secret letter from his friends' cabin.
g. Hamlet .... a new letter to the English King.
h. The branch .... and Ophelia fell into the river.
i. Hamlet did not .... that Ophelia was dead.
j. The Queen .... flowers into the grave.
k. The Queen .... from the cup.

Be going to and will

We can use **be going to** + **verb** or **will** + **verb** to talk about the future.
We generally use **be going to**:

- to talk about a fixed plan
  For example: ***I'm going to fly** to New York next Monday.*
- when we are sure that something is going to happen
  For example: *Look at the black clouds. **It's going to rain**.*

We generally use **will**:

- when we have an idea at the moment of speaking about the future
  For example: *Look. The sun is shining. **I'll go** to the beach.*

We often use short forms in speaking:
I'll/he'll/they'll etc.
I'm going to / she's going to / they're going to etc.

4 **Complete the sentences 1-10 by using *is/are going to* or *will*. Use short forms.**

   0. I've got an idea! Let's perform *Hamlet*. I .ll.act...................... the part of Horatio.

  00. Look at this poster. Next month, the Royal Shakespeare Company .is.going.to.............. act here.

   1. Look! The Ghost is coming. I .... ask it some questions.

   2. 'Where are you going?' 'I .... tell Hamlet about the Ghost.'

   3. How can I trick Claudius? I know! I .... behave as if I'm crazy.

   4. This is the plan. Ophelia .... meet Hamlet in the hall.

   5. 'What's the rest of your plan?' 'We .... listen to their conversation.'

   6. 'Why are the actors here?' 'They .... perform a play for the King.'

   7. I've got an idea. We .... use poison to kill Hamlet.

   8. The Queen drank the poison. She .... die soon.

   9. Come to the castle. Horatio .... explain everything at a special meeting.

  10. All right, I .... come with you to the meeting.

5 After the bells, you will hear some famous lines from Shakespeare's original play. (Remember: Shakespeare wrote 400 years ago, so the language is old-fashioned and difficult!) Which character is speaking? Can you decide at which moment in the story?

a. Frailty,* thy name is woman.
Frailty : Fragility.

b. Something is rotten* in the state of Denmark.
rotten : bad, wrong.

c. Adieu,* adieu, adieu. Remember me.
Adieu : Goodbye.

d. ... one may smile and smile, and be a villain—*
villain : bad man (the opposite of 'hero').

e. The play's the thing
Wherein* I'll catch the conscience of the King.
Wherein : In which.

f. To be, or not to be, that is the question:

g. Madness in great ones must not unwatch'd go.

h. Suit the action to the word, the word to the action, ...*
Suit ... action, ... : Make your performance appropriate to the play.

i. My words fly up, my thoughts remain below.
Words without thoughts never to heaven go.

j. How now? A rat! Dead for a ducat,* dead.
ducat : silver coin.

k. Thou turn'st* my eyes into my very soul,
Thou turn'st : You turn.

l. Sweet ladies, good night, good night.

m. Alas, poor Yorick. I knew him, Horatio–

n. There's a divinity that shapes our ends,*
There's ... ends... : a god which controls our lives.

o. The rest is silence.

6 **Do you want to act the play?**

THE SCRIPT:
You can use this story as a script for a performance of the story of *Hamlet*.
A narrator reads the descriptions.
Actors read the parts in the speech bubbles.

ROLES:
You need 8 people to play the parts of: HAMLET

CLAUDIUS

GERTRUDE

THE GHOST

HORATIO

OPHELIA

POLONIUS

LAERTES

You also need: A NARRATOR
You need more actors to play the parts of :   ROSENCRANTZ AND

GUILDENSTERN

THE GUARDS

THE PLAYERS

Remember   One actor can play more than one part.

Girls can take male parts or vice versa. Remember that in
Shakespeare's time, boys always played the female parts!

Different people can take the part of the Narrator.

SCENERY:
You can make your own scenery. Use a large piece of paper and coloured
pens or paints to make a picture of the towers of Elsinore Castle. Fix it on the
back wall of your classroom or stage.
You can make cardboard swords for the fight between Laertes and Hamlet.
Use classroom chairs for the thrones of Gertrude and Claudius.

ACTING:

Practise speaking the lines. Your teacher can help you to pronounce the lines correctly and with emotion.

Think about where to stand and how to move.

Think about the expressions on your face – is your character happy, angry, calm, upset, sad?

THE PERFORMANCE:

You can act only one part of the play and read from your books.

OR

You can learn the parts and act the whole play from beginning to end.

You can act a part of the play for other students in your class.

OR

You can act the whole play for the rest of your school or for your friends and family.

PROGRAMME AND POSTERS:

You can advertise the play to other students by designing posters.

You can write a programme for the audience. Write a paragraph about Shakespeare and about the story. Make a list of the actors. Write a paragraph about the reasons why you enjoy the play.

ENJOY ACTING THE PLAY!!!

Who was Hamlet?

Where did the story of Hamlet begin?

There is an old document about the history of Denmark. The name of the writer is Saxo Grammaticus and he lived in the twelfth century. That was more than four hundred years before Shakespeare. Saxo writes the story of a king and queen of Denmark and their son, Amleth. The king's brother murders him and marries the queen. Amleth wants revenge. He behaves like a fool, so the new king does not think that he is dangerous. He kills a friend of the bad king. Finally, he kills the bad king. In this legend, the prince does not die. He becomes a great soldier and leader. He marries a beautiful Scottish queen. The story has a happy ending! This is different from Shakespeare's drama.

Even before the time of Saxo Grammaticus, there are some poems from Iceland which tell a similar story. We don't know the date of these.

Much later, in 1570, a French author wrote about this story. The writer's name was Francois de Belleforest. A few years after this, an English dramatist, [1] Thomas Kyd, wrote a play about Hamlet. We think that Shakespeare liked the story and decided to write his play, *Hamlet, Prince of Denmark*. He changed a lot of things in the story. Shakespeare's Prince Hamlet is very intelligent and thinks about life and death in a new way.

The title page of Saxo Grammaticus' history of Denmark, published in Paris in 1514

---

1. **dramatist** : someone who writes plays.

Where is Hamlet's castle?

The name of Hamlet's castle is Elsinore. This is a place in Denmark. Shakespeare didn't go to Denmark but he knew the story of Prince Hamlet. Nowadays in Elsinore (which the Danes now call Helsingør), you can see a fantastic old castle. The name is Kronberg Slot. But it is not Hamlet's castle. The real Hamlet lived many centuries before they built this castle. Sometimes, they act Shakespeare's play in Kronberg Slot. It is a wonderful thing to see.

A view of Kronberg Slot, Hamlet's castle

A scene from *Search Hamlet,* a modern performance based on *Hamlet* acted in Kronberg Slot

93

1 Complete the table by writing items from the box in the correct place. Write the items in the correct chronological order.

date unknown   1570

late sixteenth century   late sixteenth century

a story by Belleforest   Icelandic poems

Shakespeare's *Hamlet*   a history by Saxo Grammaticus

Thomas Kyd's *Hamlet*   twelfth century

THE STORY OF HAMLET	
Date	Story
(1)	(2)
(3)	(4)
(5)	(6)
(7)	(8)
(9)	(10)

2 Now choose the right answers to these questions.

1. Who wrote the first story about the prince?
   A ☐ Shakespeare
   B ☐ Saxo Grammaticus
   C ☐ Thomas Kyd

2. What is the big difference in the story of *Amleth* from the story of Shakespeare's *Hamlet*?
   A ☐ The prince doesn't die at the end.
   B ☐ Hamlet kills the bad king.
   C ☐ The bad king kills Hamlet's father.

3. What is the name of the castle in Helsingør?
   A ☐ Elsinore.
   B ☐ Kronberg Slot.
   C ☐ Hamlet's Castle.

1 **Answer the questions below. For each question, mark the letter next to the correct answer – A, B, C or D.**

1. Which of these problems is NOT one of Hamlet's problems in the play?

   A ☐ His uncle murdered his father.

   B ☐ His mother married his father's killer.

   C ☐ His girlfriend's father and his friends spied on him.

   D ☐ The Ghost did not tell the truth.

2. What did Hamlet plan to do?

   A ☐ To kill Claudius while he was praying.

   B ☐ To kill Polonius.

   C ☐ To use the play to find out the truth.

   D ☐ To marry Ophelia.

3. Why did Claudius really send Hamlet to England?

   A ☐ To punish him for killing Polonius.

   B ☐ As part of a plan to kill him.

   C ☐ To find work for Rosencrantz and Guildenstern.

   D ☐ To please the Queen.

4. What did Hamlet do when he returned from the journey to England?

   A ☐ He sent a letter to Claudius.

   B ☐ He visited Ophelia.

   C ☐ He asked Laertes to fight him.

   D ☐ He went to the Queen's bedroom.

5. Which of the following is the best description of the end of the play?

   A ☐ There is a fight between Hamlet and Laertes. Hamlet wins, but also dies.

   B ☐ The Queen tries to save Hamlet but dies before she can do this.

   C ☐ The plans of Claudius and Laertes go wrong and finally Hamlet takes revenge.

   D ☐ Shakespeare shows that it is bad to take revenge.

2 **Here are some opinions about Hamlet's character and actions. In each box, write**

A	if you agree
D	if you disagree
?	if you are not sure...

a. Hamlet waited too long to kill Claudius.

b. He was a murderer.

c. He was cruel to Ophelia.

d. He was wrong not to believe the Ghost immediately.

e. He caused Ophelia's death.

f. He was jealous of the relationship between his mother and Claudius.

g. After he saw the Ghost, his life changed.

h. He was *really* mad. He wasn't pretending.

i. He was a hero.

j. He did his best in a difficult situation.

3 **Change the ending of *Hamlet!* Write your version.**

Example:
- Claudius stops Gertrude from drinking the poison
- The lords and ladies ask why
- They discover that the drink is poisoned
- They realise Claudius is a murderer
- Hamlet tells them that Claudius murdered King Hamlet
- Claudius confesses
- The guards take Claudius away
- Hamlet becomes the new king

Write the dialogue for your new ending.

Example:

CLAUDIUS: Gertrude, don't drink from that cup!

FIRST LORD: Why did he stop her from drinking?

SECOND LORD: It's very strange. Perhaps there is something in the drink...

2-3 Open answers.

1 1.D 2.C 3.B 4.A 5.C

Key to Exit Test